Celebrating Our Family
THROUGH THE SEASONS

RUTHANN WINANS & LINDA LEE

Illustrations by
LILA ROSE KENNEDY

HARVEST HOUSE PUBLISHERS
Eugene, Oregon

DEDICATION

*To our children, Dusty, Ashley, JJ,
and the newest addition to the Winans family, Summer Rose
Brianne, Heather, and Jared Lee
You make all our seasons delightful!*

A SPECIAL THANKS TO...

*Bob and Emilie Barnes
For your inspiration, encouragement, and friendship.*

Celebrating Our Family

Copyright © 1999 Ruthann Winans and Linda Lee
Published by Harvest House Publishers
Eugene, Oregon 97402

ISBN 1-56507-909-4

Artwork designs are reproduced under license from © Arts Uniq' ®, Inc., Cookeville, TN and may not be reproduced without permission. For information regarding art prints featured in this book, please contact:

Arts Uniq'
P.O. Box 3085
Cookeville, TN 38502
800-223-5020

Design and production by Garborg Design Works, Minneapolis, Minnesota

Unless otherwise indicated, Scripture quotations are from the Holy Bible, New Living Translation © 1996. Used by permission of Tyndale House Publishers, Inc., 60189. All rights reserved.

Printed in China.

99 00 01 02 03 04 05 06 07 08 / IM / 10 9 8 7 6 5 4 3 2 1

Contents

Celebrating Our Family

is a celebration of the seasons of family life—*your* family's life! It is a very special keepsake album in which you and your family tell the delightful story of this time in your life together.

Within the pages of this album you will discover how simple it is to create your own family heirloom. You'll find charming stories, homey quotes, and easy memory-making ideas to motivate and inspire you throughout the seasons. Every section offers you new ways to personalize the album to make it uniquely your own. Look for topical photo spots where you may highlight one special photo or a collage of cropped photos. Take a moment to jot down a short response to the journal prompts. Create a truly memorable scrapbook page with an acid-free glue stick and a few family mementos: love notes, postcards, ticket stubs, or crayon drawings.

You'll find that it only takes a bit of time here and there to create a lasting keepsake of your family's life. Don't let another priceless moment pass you by! Begin today—no matter what season it is. Begin to tell your family's story. You'll be so glad you did!

May *Celebrating Our Family* bring delight to all your seasons and may it become a keepsake that will be treasured for generations to come!

From Our Families to Yours,
Ruthann and Linda

We treasure this photo of our happy family—

It's a loving remembrance of the life that we now lead,

It's a fleeting moment captured for posterity.

It reminds us to cherish the seasons yet to be.

(PLACE FAMILY PHOTO HERE.)

This Is Our Story...

Four Delightful Seasons in the Life of the _____ Family!

From the _____ of _____ to the _____ of _____.

SEASON YOU BEGAN YOUR RECORD   YEAR   SEASON YOU ENDED YOUR RECORD   YEAR

Berries 'n' Blossoms

Roused from winter's silent slumber, a drowsy earth yawns and stretches beneath the welcoming grin of spring. The joyful season of new beginnings has arrived!

Butter yellow rays of toasty warm sunlight break the icy grip of winter on the land, sending laughing brooks on an unexpected roller-coaster ride. Cheery azure skies invite tender, green shoots to come out and play. Soft breezes gently coax fragrant blossoms into exhaling their sweet perfume. Curly,

brown vines, expectant with the promise of blushing berries, delight in refreshing spring showers. Even the most stubborn trees can't resist joining in spring's jubilant celebration of life. They gladly unfold their ornate leaves for tiny bird families who embellish the lush woodland canopy with happy songs of the season.

Spring brings a fresh outlook to the seasons of our life. It revitalizes our perspective, painting our winter gray world with luxurious color. It arouses our drowsy senses with a splendid

Under the windows is my garden, where sweet, sweet flowers grow,
and in the pear tree dwells a robin, the dearest bird I know.
KATE GREENAWAY

profusion of invigorating sounds, fragrances, and tastes. Even in its simplest moments, spring works miracles, softening the hardest hearts with little more than an armful of squirming newborn pups covered in downy-soft fur.

It's no wonder we eagerly await the birth of spring each year. Like expectant parents, we long to hug this smiling, cooing infant of a season—to revel in its innocence and sweetness. And spring, the ever-energetic toddler, tugs at us and begs us to explore with enthusiastic abandon this masterpiece of creation we lovingly call home. It stirs our emotions, captures our heart, and restores the precious gift of childlike wonder to us. And so, refreshed by spring, we fall hopelessly in love with life once more.

The wonderful thing about spring is...

_____

_____

_____

_____

_____

_____

_____

Spring Delights!

Fly a kite.

Plant Sweet Peas. Their aroma is "heaven scent"!

Blow bubbles on a breezy day.

Tie flower stems together and make a homey blossom necklace

Go berry picking.

Gather fresh flowers to bring indoors.

Hang a bird feeder in front of the kitchen window.

Spring Treasures...

Let's stroll along the garden path,

Where the air smells sweet and green,

What lovely blossoms flourish there,

Wondrous treasures of the season!

(PLACE PHOTO HERE.)

This is our favorite place to stop and smell the roses.

_____

_____

_____

The earth laughs in flowers.
RALPH WALDO EMERSON

A Gathering of Spring Blessings!

Gather together a few treasured symbols of spring. Display them as "Spring Blessings" with little trimmings on a small table top or decorative tray.

- A square of colorful cloth is a nice background for this display.

- An antique vase or pitcher makes a lovely container for delicate spring blossoms. Look through the attic or search local flea markets and garage sales for a new "family heirloom."

- A collage of photos: puppies, kittens, colts, and lambs.

- A small grapevine wreath decorated with assorted buttons and stuffed with raffia makes a whimsical nest for a collection of wooden eggs. Have the children paint a Mama and Papa bird to stand guard over the nest.

- A children's picture book with a spring theme makes a charming backdrop, and reading it together is a fun family activity for the season.

- A glass canning jar is the perfect place to display rocks and other treasures collected on leisurely walks. Set a magnifying glass near it for taking a closer look.

- Include a handwritten family love note. Make it a point to talk about the nicest blessing of all—being a family together. Proudly display the note as a springtime blessing. (Use the space below to record a few lines from the note.)

Being a family is the nicest blessing of all!

_____

_____

_____

Our Spring Favorites

- Berry_____
- Garden Flower_____
- Baby Animal_____
- Place to Walk to_____
- Riddle or Joke_____

  _____
- After-School Activity_____

  _____
- Snack_____
- Television Show_____

Here's What's Cookin'

Angel Berry Cloud Cake

- *angel food cake (store bought or homemade)*
- *sliced strawberries (fresh and lightly sweetened with sugar, or frozen)*
- *vanilla ice cream*
- *whipped cream*

Fold sliced strawberries into softened ice cream. Place a generous scoop onto a slice of angel food cake. Top with a dollop of whipped cream. Garnish with a fresh strawberry dipped in melted chocolate for an extra special treat.

Light as a cloud and loaded with berries—this angel food cake is heavenly!

Yummy!

SPRING

But friendship is precious, not only in the shade, but in the sunshine of life; and thanks to a benevolent arrangement of things, the greater part of life is sunshine.

THOMAS JEFFERSON

The Best of Friends

Good friends are like Baby Bear's porridge...they are "just right!"

They know how to do really important things—

things like how to keep a secret, share a laugh, and give a hug.

(PLACE PHOTO HERE.)

Friends we like to spend time with..._____

_____

A few things we like to do together..._____

_____

_____

_____

The Royal Treatment

Everyone deserves the royal treatment sometimes. Get the family together to create a regal crown to celebrate royal occasions. Fashion a crown from poster board. Cover it with tin foil then decorate it with braid and craft store "gems." (Fancy is good—outrageous is better!) Use the crown as a royal honor for: birthdays, Mother's and Father's Day, good grades, or good deeds. Take a photo of a loved one getting the royal treatment. It will be a keepsake that's fit for a king!

There is no charm so great as the charm of a cheerful temperament.

HENRY VAN DYKE

Family Charms!

Just a word or two to describe what is most charming about our family... _____

_____

_____

_____

_____

_____

Our Spring Memories...

(PLACE MEMENTOS HERE.)

We picked some posies, just one or two,
They were lovely ladies through and through,
Gently pressed—preserved by time,
They'll be a garden of remembrance when spring subsides.

LINDA LEE

Sleeping Angels

The quiet hours have come at last,

One bear hug and a kiss goodnight —

Sleep in peace little angel!

(PLACE PHOTO HERE.)

Heart to Heart...

This spring we shared a special moment that I'll always treasure. _____

_____

_____

_____

_____ Love,

_____ *Mom*

Now the world is sleeping,
little stars are peeping,
Father, in Thy keeping,
may my children rest.

UNKNOWN

Hand Hugs!

Preserve precious handprints on this keepsake page. Outline each child's hand using different colored markers, then label them. It's a hand hug to treasure forever!

Spring Is Popping Up All Over!

Egg-stra Fun!

When the weather begins to warm, call the family outdoors to play these games.

🍃 **EGG TOSS:** Choose partners or stand in a circle, and then toss an uncooked egg back and forth. Try not to break it. After each round, increase the distance between players to make the game more challenging. Have the camera ready to capture the surprised looks and laughter when the egg finally breaks.

🍃 **EGG ROLLING:** Since 1878 children have been invited to roll eggs on the White House lawn. Try holding an egg rolling race in the family backyard. See who can roll an egg the farthest without breaking it!

Family Tidbits and Trivia

Our ancestors came from these countries...

_____

_____

This is the place where we've lived the longest...

_____

Here is an Easter tradition that has been passed down through our family... _____

_____

_____

_____

Cozy rooms and homemade treasures,

Loving words and simple pleasures—

That's what makes our

"Home Sweet Home."

(PLACE PHOTO HERE.)

Home Is Where Our Heart Is!

Our favorite room in our home is _____

This is what we like best about it _____

_____

Our most prized family heirloom is _____

It can be found in this room in our home _____

We get the best view of spring from this spot in our home _____

_____

Springtime Joys

- Create a sidewalk garden with colorful chalk and lots of imagination. Include mile-high sunflowers, berries by the bushel, and lots of bunny food—carrots!

- Secretly leave a May Basket on a neighbor's doorstep.

- Little hands can easily decorate Easter eggs with non-toxic colored markers.

- Make festive speckled Easter eggs by using a bit of natural sea sponge dipped in coloring to press a pattern onto an egg. (Use a clothespin to hold onto the sponge and to keep fingers cleaner.)

- Go on an Easter egg hunt. Mark several eggs with a smiley face—the one who finds them gets a prize.

- Attend an Easter sunrise service.

- Decorate a special apron just for Mom this Mother's Day. Children can dip their hands in paint and press them along the hemline of the apron to create "handmade lace." Use novelty buttons to create fancy jewelry for your handprints. Then embellish them with names, ages, and loving sentiments.

Happy Birthday, Dear...

Guess who had a birthday!

_____

We celebrated by _____

_____

A Birthday Wish _____

_____

Guess who had a birthday!

_____

We celebrated by _____

_____

A Birthday Wish _____

_____

Let's Celebrate Life!

(Place mementos here.)

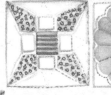

Watermelon 'n' Fireflies

The first hurrah of summer comes strutting into town like a proud band marching to a Sousa beat. And what a delightful cacophony of activity it brings: good, old-fashioned family picnics at the park, down-home county fairs, picturesque camping trips, impromptu neighborhood baseball games, trips to the seashore, and unabashed displays of patriotism with fireworks for exclamation points.

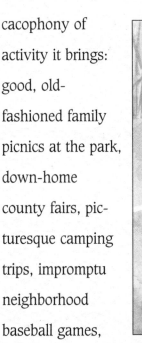

Just throw open the kitchen window and the sounds of summer come tumbling in on warm breezes, filling the house with the joyful exuberance of children playing, dogs barking, hoses hissing, and mowers whirring.

Then just when it's least expected, the happy din dissolves to a whisper, and the hearts of all turn to the quiet pleasures of summer—the taste of crisp, sweet, smiling wedges of watermelon and the feel of velvety warm sand underfoot.

When one has tasted watermelon he knows what the angels eat.

MARK TWAIN

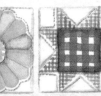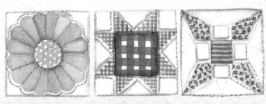

The young begin to yearn for the solitary work of making daisy-chain necklaces and skipping smooth, round stones neatly across the surface of the lake. The old long for the sway of a hammock and the company of a good book.

During the quiet days of summer, adventure is finding a daydream in puffy marshmallow clouds that amble across the sky. And at the end of a perfectly quiet summer day? Well, nothing could be finer than having front-porch seats for the light show the fireflies graciously provide each evening.

Summer feeds the soul of the seasons of our life with a nourishing contrast of excitement and respite. From the abundance of its pantry come some of the fondest childhood memories. Blessed is the child whose longings are satisfied with summertime pleasures.

The wonderful thing about summer is...

_____

_____

_____

_____

_____

_____

_____

Summer Delights!

Go fishing.

Catch fireflies.

Spit watermelon seeds for distance.

Play in the sprinklers!

Sing silly songs on long car trips.

Roast marshmallows over a blazing campfire.

Enjoy a root beer float for dessert under the twinkling stars. Don't forget to make a wish!

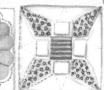

Good Old Summertime...

A county fair, a family picnic,
A good book, a dip in a cool stream—
We love these leisurely pastimes!

(PLACE PHOTO HERE.)

This is our favorite way to spend a leisurely summer day!

_____

_____

_____

Summer afternoon—summer afternoon...to me those have
always been the two most beautiful words in the English language.

HENRY JAMES

Oh, for a little time to enjoy the beauties around me!
Just a little while to be free of the tyranny of things that must be done!
LAURA INGALLS WILDER

Golden Wishes

The long, lazy days of summer seem to linger on slowly until August arrives. Then the thought hits: Only four more weeks until school starts, and we haven't done everything we wanted to do yet! (Where does the time go?)

This summer, give each family member one golden wish. This wish is to be spent on one activity that will make the summer really memorable for that person. The only rule is that the wish can't cost a bag of gold!

After compiling the list of golden wishes, put gold stars on the calendar to mark the days when those wishes will come true. Once a wish has been granted, jot down a highlight or two in this album. These will be solid gold memories for sure!

Golden wishes we made this summer...

_____

_____

_____

_____

_____

_____

_____

_____

_____

Our Summer Favorites

🌿 Vacation Getaway _____

🌿 Picnic Spot _____

🌿 Fishing Hole _____

🌿 Way to Cool Off _____

🌿 Place to Think _____

🌿 Song to Sing Around the Campfire _____

_____

🌿 Game to Play on Long Car Rides _____

🌿 Food to Barbecue _____

🌿 Houseguest _____

🌿 Movie _____

Front Porch Ice Cream Sandwiches

- *To a favorite waffle batter recipe add 2 tablespoons sugar.*
- *Prepare waffles and let them cool.*
- *Dip the edge of each waffle square in warm white or dark chocolate.*
- *After the chocolate dries, scoop a favorite ice cream (slightly softened) onto one waffle square and top with another square.*
- *Sprinkle with a light dusting of powdered sugar.*
- *Serve right away.*

Tastes best when eaten while sitting on a squeaky old porch swing!

Fun in the Sun!

A baseball game, a nature hike,
a long bike ride—this is how we like to play.

(PLACE PHOTO HERE.)

When it's time to go outdoors and play these are the things we like
to do! _____

_____

_____

_____

Family Super Bowl

Create a bowling alley in the backyard with just 10 empty plastic soda or water bottles and a ball. Set the bowling pins in the traditional "V" formation. Mark the starting point with a chalk line, and then let 'er roll! Play for points or just play for fun.

Kids say and do the funniest things!

Here is something that tickled our funny bone: _____

_____

_____

_____

_____

_____

_____

_____

_____

_____

Our Summer Memories...

(PLACE MEMENTOS HERE.)

We gathered up postcards and wrapped them with twine,
We pocketed seashells washed in with the tide,
We treasured them often as time passed by,
Blessed memories of summertimes spent side-by-side.

LINDA LEE

Giggles and Smiles!

Knock-knock jokes and
Funny faces, silly stories
And ticklish embraces—
We love making each other smile!

(PLACE PHOTO HERE.)

A good laugh is sunshine in a house.

WILLIAM MAKEPEACE THACKERAY

Laugh Lines

This is the joke that makes us laugh most: _____

_____

_____

_____

_____

_____

Our Summer Getaway

*The true way to live is to enjoy each moment
as it passes, and surely it is in the everyday things around us
that the beauty of life lies.*

LAURA INGALLS WILDER

This is a drawing of our family on vacation at _____

by: _____ age: _____

When we are on vacation we love to _____

_____

_____

_____

Sunny Days Are Here Again!

Bubbles for Fun in the Sun!

This is a best-ever bubble recipe.

> *6 cups water*
> *2 cups "Joy" liquid dish soap*
> *3/4 cup clear Karo corn syrup*

Mix together thoroughly.

❦ Dip a kitchen funnel into the mixture and blow gently through the narrow opening.

❦ Create jumbo bubble shapes with a homemade bubble wand. Bend a wire coat hanger into a desired shape then bend the hook into a handle. Dip the wand into a large pan of bubble solution then slowly swish it through the air to make super giant bubbles.

❦ Try to catch the bubbles in a pie tin or plate!

Family Tidbits and Trivia

A family heirloom that we treasure..._____

_____

A saying we love to quote..._____

_____

Something we hope to never forget..._____

_____

A man travels the world over in search of what he needs and returns home to find it.

GEORGE MOORE

Enchanting places near and far.

We've seen them all from the family car.

(PLACE PHOTO HERE.)

Our Family Car

Year _____ Model _____

A Pajamas and Ice Cream Surprise!

On a warm summer evening, just after the kids have dressed for bed, ring a bell and announce that everyone is to pile into the car and take a drive into town for an ice-cream surprise...pajamas and all!

Celebrate Summer

🐚 Add a splash of fun to a summer afternoon. Play catch with water balloons.

🐚 Read stories outside under a shady tree while sitting on a comfy quilt.

🐚 Lie on the grass, look up at the clouds, and make up a fairy tale, happy ending and all.

🐚 Go on a garage sale treasure hunt. Look for tiny things to fill a show-and-tell basket. Bring the basket out when your summer guests come to visit. It's a great conversation starter!

🐚 No one can fill Dad's shoes, but on Father's Day it would be fun to try! Fill Dad's shoes with love notes and wrapped candies, then watch for the look on his face when he bends down to put them on.

🐚 On the Fourth of July, make it a tradition to sing patriotic songs and say the Pledge of Allegiance while on the way to view fireworks.

This is the name of our President: _____

Happy Birthday, Dear...

Guess who had a birthday!

_____

We celebrated by _____

_____

A Birthday Wish _____

_____

Guess who had a birthday!

_____

We celebrated by _____

_____

A Birthday Wish _____

_____

Hip–Hip–Hurray!
It's Independence Day!

(PLACE MEMENTOS HERE.)

Pumpkins 'n' Popcorn

Fall approaches with the steady ease and confidence of a kindly grandma. She patiently waits her turn, content to let the seasons of youth have their days of glory. Distracted by youthful endeavors, summer doesn't even notice the coming of fall until he begins to take a chill. Then he reluctantly waves goodbye as his summer playground is prepared for the harvest.

With able hands, Grandma Autumn dresses the landscape before her. Rolling green hills are instructed to put on their warm, brown coats. Stately trees heave a sigh of relief, then willingly let crisp fall winds relieve them of their heavy load, leaving a lush, leafy carpet of gold around their feet. Roadside stands are laden with dreams come true: bushels of ripe, red apples, firm gourds, and amber-colored honey.

Ahh...the simple pleasures of autumn: bright orange pumpkins, the scent of wood smoke in the air, buttery popcorn, flame colored leaves, hot spiced cider, and a thankful harvest homecoming.

RUTHANN WINANS

But fall's most coveted offering adorns the field, where regal cornstalks stand like silent sentries, watching over their prized bounty. There, proud and robust pumpkins sit nestled in among the curly vines and bales of sweet scented hay like jewels in a crown—just waiting to become the delight of giggling children.

Fall heralds the end of the growing season, yet it also ushers in the beginning of a season of thankfulness. It is a heartfelt thankfulness that grows from the understanding that life itself is a blessing. And so with friends and family gathered around the Thanksgiving table, we give our thanks: thanks for the blessing of the harvest, for food, shelter, and clothing; thanks for the blessing of God and country; and thanks for the blessing of another season together. In doing so, we add the grace and beauty of thankfulness to the seasons of our life.

The wonderful thing about fall is...

_____

_____

_____

_____

_____

_____

_____

_____

Fall Delights!

❧

Bundle up for a harvest hayride.

❧

Visit the pumpkin patch—the perfect setting for fall pictures.

❧

Roast pumpkin seeds.

❧

Bring the harvest home. Decorate a mantel or shelf with pumpkins, gourds, Indian corn, colorful leaves, pine branches, shiny red apples, and nuts.

❧

Set out an old-fashioned chalkboard and as a family make a list of things to give thanks for.

Pick of the Crop

The bounty of the harvest overflowing from baskets

At a farmer's market,

Robust pumpkins tucked among curly vines—

We love these autumn pleasures!

(PLACE PHOTO HERE.)

When the air turns crisp and leaves begin to fall, these are the autumn pleasures we look forward to most of all! _____

_____

_____

_____

_____

Gather the golden pumpkins,
Climb for the rosy apples,
Dig for the brown potatoes,
For harvest time is here!

FRENCH FOLK SONG

Autumn Keepsakes

A Leaf Rubbing

Take a leisurely walk and collect fall leaves. Preserve their graceful image for this album by making a leaf rubbing.

Place a leaf, vein side up, on a hard surface. Lay a sheet of paper over it. Hold a colored pencil at an angle and rub the paper until the outline of the leaf appears. Once complete, trim the leaf shapes with scissors. Then glue your autumn keepsakes onto this scrapbook page.

This is where we collected our leaves... _____

_____

Our Fall Favorites

🍎 Place to See Fall Color _____

🍎 First Day of School Breakfast _____

🍎 Book to Read by Candlelight _____

🍎 Pumpkin Patch _____

🍎 Autumn Dessert _____

🍎 Traditional Mealtime Blessing _____

_____

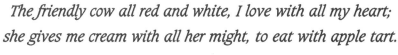

Apple Wedges & Warm Vanilla Caramel Sauce

TRY THIS DELICIOUS AUTUMN TREAT.

- On a platter, arrange crisp green apple wedges.
- In the center, place a bowl of warmed caramel sauce to which a teaspoon of vanilla extract has been added. Purchase the sauce, or try this recipe:

In a double boiler melt...

50 caramel candies	1 tablespoon butter
2 tablespoons milk	1 teaspoon vanilla extract

Tastes especially yummy when served with a glass of ice cold milk.

The friendly cow all red and white, I love with all my heart;
she gives me cream with all her might, to eat with apple tart.

ROBERT LOUIS STEVENSON

School Days!

Smiling faces, fresh beginning,

Greeting friends both old and new—

That's what we look forward to on the first day of school.

(PLACE PHOTO HERE.)

NAME   GRADE   SCHOOL

Family Jam Session

During the harvest season, serve a hearty helping of appetizing food for thought to inspire family dialogue around the supper table.

❦ Write down one word conversation topics on small slips of paper. Try a variety of topics: honesty, bravery, joy, love, truth, compassion, fun, travel, favorites, food, heaven, history, angels, future, sports, beach, mountains, etc.

❦ Place the topics in a bowl or basket and then pass it around the table. Give each person a few minutes to talk about whatever comes to mind when the topic is read.

Whatever is true...noble... right...pure... lovely...admirable —if anything is excellent or praiseworthy— think about such things.

THE BOOK OF PHILIPPIANS

Family Tidbits and Trivia

Someday we'll have fun remembering our favorite brands and how "cheap" things used to be...

Peanut Butter _____ $ _____

Coffee _____ $ _____

Ice Cream _____ $ _____

Cereal _____ $ _____

Loaf of Bread _____ $ _____

Laundry Soap _____ $ _____

Shampoo _____ $ _____

Average Cost of Groceries for the Week $ _____

Item We Always Run Out of First _____

Gather 'Round...

There are few things we love better,

When the day at last is through,

Than to gather around the table,

For a meal and conversation, too!

(PLACE PHOTO HERE.)

The meal we love the most is _____

_____

A Favorite Family Recipe _____

_____

_____

_____

_____

_____

Autumn Is in the Air!

Housewarmings...

Here are some ways to make a home warm and cozy when the weather turns blustery.

- At the first sign of chilly weather, light a fire.
- No fireplace? Light a vanilla scented candle!
- Spiced apple cider will fill a home with the delicious aroma of fall. Keep it simmering in a slow-cooker all day long, and it will be a warm welcome home to dear ones coming in from the cold.

> 1 gallon apple cider   10 whole cloves
> 1 cup brown sugar   1 sliced orange

Set a "mitten basket" near the door, and fill it with one size fits all stretch knit gloves. *They'll warm hearts as well as hands!*

Happy Birthday, Dear...

Guess who had a birthday!   Guess who had a birthday!

_____   _____

We celebrated by_____   We celebrated by_____

_____   _____

A Birthday Wish_____   A Birthday Wish_____

_____   _____

Come ye thankful people come,
Raise the song of harvest home,
All is safely gathered in,
Ere the winter storms begin.

HENRY ALFORD

Pumpkins, leaves, and cornstalks tall,
That's how we decorate our home for fall!

(PLACE PHOTO HERE.)

Home for the Harvest

Our address _____

We've lived here since _____

In our home, we celebrate fall by _____

_____

_____

_____

Thankful Hearts

Express gratitude in a unique way this Thanksgiving. As a family, decorate a small pine tree with colorful fall leaves and delightfully scented cinnamon heart ornaments. Embellish the ornaments with words that represent what the family is most thankful for.

| Love | Faith | Friends | Freedom |
| Health | Family | Food | Home |

We are most thankful for... _____

_____

_____

Cinnamon Heart Ornaments

1 cup ground cinnamon
4 tablespoons white glue
3/4 cup water

Mix until it is the consistency of cookie dough. (Add more water if needed.) Sprinkle cinnamon on the cutting board and knead dough. Roll out 1/4-inch thick. Cut out with a heart-shaped cookie cutter. Punch a hole in the top with a straw before drying. Bake in 350° oven for 30 minutes or until firm. Let them cool, then decorate!

Write words of thankfulness on each heart using pearl white T-shirt paint. Outline the edge with painted dots or dashes. Sprinkle with iridescent glitter for a sugary look. After the paint is dry, use a bit of raffia, ribbon, or torn strips of calico to tie the ornaments to the tree.

Turkey and Trimmings!

The delicious aroma of turkey baking,

Watch as Grandma gives it one more basting,

A tasty feast is finally spread,

Then with thankful hearts we bow our heads.

(PLACE PHOTO HERE.)

Our traditional Thanksgiving menu...

_____

_____

_____

_____

_____

_____

A Thoughtful Tradition

Add this thoughtful tradition to your Thanksgiving celebration this year. Cut autumn leaf shapes out of paper. On each leaf write a thought on the topic of thankfulness. Use quotes, Scriptures, or write a short sentence describing a time when the family was most grateful. Set a leaf at each place setting. Then at different times throughout the meal ask someone to read a "Grateful Thought" out loud.

Our favorite grateful thought is... _____

_____

_____

45

Pin the Feather on the Turkey

🍂 Outline the shape of a turkey without feathers on a piece of poster board.

🍂 Give younger ones crayons to color the turkey.

🍂 Let older ones cut feather shapes from colored paper.

🍂 Players write what they are thankful for on the feather, then put a piece of double stick tape on the back.

🍂 Blindfold players one by one, give them a spin, and watch as they try to pin the feather on the turkey!

Gobble, Gobble...

Thanksgiving traditions that we enjoy year after year... _____

_____

_____

_____

_____

_____

_____

Hurrah for the fun! Is the turkey done? Hurrah for the pumpkin pie!

LYDIA MARIA CHILD

A Bountiful and Happy Thanksgiving Day!

(PLACE MEMENTOS HERE.)

It is good to give thanks...

THE BOOK OF PSALMS

Jingle Bells 'n' Candlelight

Like the bright star that shone over Bethlehem, Christmas is the shining star of the winter season. It shines like a beacon of light in the darkness, beckoning all hearts to return to the comforting embrace of home.

At Christmastime, more than any other season, our thoughts turn toward home. The cheerful jangle of jingle bells signaling the arrival of friends at the door, the happy bedlam that accompanies the joyful

homecoming of loved ones, the sweet harmonies of sentimental carols sung around the piano, the reassuring cadence of age-old stories faithfully read—these are the heart-warming sounds of home.

The invigorating smell of hot spiced cider, the rich aroma of gingerbread baking in the oven, the pine-scented goodness of a freshly cut Christmas tree—these are the familiar scents of home. Rosy-cheeked children wearing angelic

Our hearts grow tender with childhood memories and love of kindred and we are better throughout the year for having in spirit become a child again at Christmastime.

LAURA INGALLS WILDER

grins, overstuffed stockings hung neatly in a row, hand-written letters from dear old friends, the kitchen table set with a delicious array of yummy treats, the soft golden glow of candlelight—these are the welcome sights of home.

Yet surely it is the light of love that shines the brightest. It is the shining light of love that always beckons us home for Christmas—home to the place where our loved ones are, home to the place where we are loved.

The wonderful thing about Christmas is... _____

_____

_____

_____

_____

_____

_____

_____

_____

Christmas Delights!

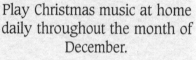

Play Christmas music at home daily throughout the month of December.

Enjoy the warm glow of candle-light with all meals during the holiday season...breakfast included!

Bundle up and go Christmas caroling in the frosty night air.

As a family, donate time or gifts to a Christmas charity that benefits children.

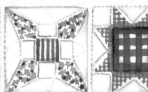

Home for the Holidays!

Our table's set with goodies sweet,

Lush garlands grace the mantle,

A shiny star for the top of our tree,

—We love getting ready for Christmas!

(Place photo here.)

It's looking a lot like Christmas around our house!
*Our most cherished holiday decorations are...*_____

Heap on more wood!
The wind is chill; but
let it whistle as it
will, we'll keep our
Christmas Merry still.

Sir Walter Scott

_____

_____

_____

_____

_____

_____

Holiday Sentiments

Add a heartwarming touch to the home this season. Decorate tabletops, centerpieces, mantels, or the Christmas tree with charming miniature chalkboards embellished with joyful holiday sentiments.

Little chalkboards can be found very inexpensively at craft stores. Write the holiday sentiments with a white paint pen. (For an easy lettering style, try stick letters with dots on the ends.) Leave the wooden border simple and natural or decorate it with twigs, silk pine branches, ribbons, buttons, or old costume jewelry.

Sweet holiday sentiments...

- There's no place like home for Christmas!
- Happy Birthday, Jesus!
- Joy to the world, the Lord is come!
- Keep Christmas in your heart.
- I believe...
- Joy
- Peace
- Love
- Only __ Days Till Christmas!

Christmas Favorites

- Carol _____
- Movie _____
- Story _____
- Aroma _____
- Place to See Christmas Lights _____
- Christmas Eve Activity _____
- Breakfast on Christmas Morning _____
- Christmas Morning Attire _____
- Traditions _____

Heart to Heart...

This Christmas we shared a moment that I will always remember... _____

_____

_____

_____

_____

Love,
Dad

Heartwarmers...

It was the policy of the good old gentleman to make his children feel that home was the happiest place in the world; and I value this delicious home-feeling as one of the choicest gifts a parent could bestow.

WASHINGTON IRVING

🖤 Gather favorite Christmas books and set them in a festively decorated basket in the family room. When the mood strikes, light a candle and enjoy an old-fashioned story hour.

🖤 Start a new tradition. Select a unique ornament to hide among the others on the tree. The first one to find it gets a special treat or privilege.

🖤 Record a festive holiday message on the answering machine.

🖤 As a family, plan a day to bake a batch of holiday memories with a favorite cookie recipe. (Time-saving tip: Have the dough prepared, chilled, and ready to roll and cut out.)

🖤 Take each child out alone on a date to the mall or downtown shops to enjoy the lights and displays. Stop for hot chocolate and share Christmas wishes.

🖤 When setting out the nativity scene, let the children act out the story with the figurines.

🖤 A "Heartwarmer" we enjoyed this Christmas _____

_____

A Very Merry Christmas Day!

What wonderful goodies there could be,

Tucked beneath our Christmas tree,

Just a few more hours and we shall see—

We can hardly wait for Christmas!

(PLACE PHOTO HERE.)

Thoughtful gifts we gave... _____

_____

_____

_____

_____

_____

_____

Angel Secrets

On December 1, secretly exchange names with each other and spend the weeks before Christmas being a "secret angel." Just like an angel, plan to help and encourage that person: make a bed, leave a cookie on their pillow, hide a note in their pocket...

On Christmas Eve, have each person try to guess the identity of their angel. Then the real angels can reveal their secret with a hug!

A Christmas to Remember

Christmas Stars

Prepare a favorite sugar cookie dough and
cut it out with a mini star cookie cutter.
Bake as directed and sprinkle with sugar.
Fill a jar to the brim with these sweet little
stars. Adorn the lid with a square of festive
fabric and a ribbon bow.
On a small tag write this verse:

The stars in the bright sky
Looked down where He lay
The little Lord Jesus
Asleep on the hay.
MARTIN LUTHER

Our Favorite Christmas Recipe _____

_____

_____

_____

_____

_____

_____

_____

_____

There is nothing quite so homey and comforting

As a mother or grandma cooking in the

Kitchen with an old-fashioned apron on.

(PLACE PHOTO HERE.)

Cookin' Up a Delicious Christmas!

These loving hands cooked our Christmas dinner _____

_____

Family and friends who joined us _____

_____

_____

These foods are traditional at our Christmas table _____

_____

Homespun Christmas Fun!

Christmas cards and pageants gay,
Childlike squeals on Christmas Day,
Of all our days so sweet and blessed,
It's Christmas that we love the best.

LINDA LEE

(PLACE MEMENTOS HERE.)

Good news from heaven the angels bring,
Glad tidings to earth they sing,
To us this day is given,
To crown us with the joy of heaven.

MARTIN LUTHER

(PLACE MEMENTOS HERE.)

WINTER

Snowflakes 'n' Mittens

Winter snuggles in like napping children tucked into a pillowy soft featherbed. Tired and weary from seasons of growth, the world is ready for the pristine silence of winter. The sky overhead gladly dims with cozy cloud cover. Colors fade to a soothing gray. And a sleepy countryside quietly pulls a winter white blanket of  snowflakes as light as angel kisses right up under its chin.

Then, in those secluded places where the timid creatures live, a tranquil lullaby begins to lightly whisper through the trees. It sends the world drifting off into the deep and dreamy sleep of winter, with the twinkle of tiny stars for a nightlight.

For those who dare to brave the chill, a sparkling white wonderland awaits them. The frozen landscape is iced like a birthday cake with snowy whipped cream frosting and icicle candles. Statuesque trees strike wooden poses like thoughtful sculptures in

---

God has given us our memories that we might have roses in December.

J.M. BARRIE

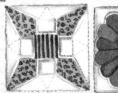

winter's museum. Stiff toboggans careen wildly down slippery slopes carrying white-knuckled youngsters on their backs. Pudgy round snowmen sporting cheesy grins and Charlie Brown Christmas tree arms cheerfully wave hello to children all bundled up in big, fat coats and wooly warm mittens.

Winter brings the gift of rest to the seasons of our life. We find it in long leisurely nights that bring sweet sleep. We luxuriate in it while sipping on mugs of rich, hot cocoa. And we discover, there in the midst of our rest, that we really do have everything we need. We have the "happily ever after" we were hoping for.

The wonderful thing about winter is...

_____

_____

_____

_____

_____

_____

_____

Cocoa Soup with Snowballs

A fun way to celebrate the first snow

❦ Prepare a favorite hot cocoa recipe.

❦ Ladle servings into soup bowls.

❦ Garnish with "snowballs"—miniature marshmallows.

Don't forget to eat this "soup" with a spoon!

Winter Delights!

Catch snowflakes the old-fashioned way—on the tip of the tongue!

Feed the birds. Spread peanut butter on a bagel then roll it in bird seed. Tie a ribbon through the center and hang it from a tree limb.

Have a snowball fight.

No snow? Have a paper snowball fight with wadded up balls of paper for snowballs.

Play board games by the glow of firelight.

Cold Hands, Warm Heart

All bundled up in our coats and hats,

We look a bit like snowmen—just think of that!

(PLACE PHOTO HERE.)

The best place to enjoy the winter weather is... _____

_____

_____

_____

Unforgettable...That's What We Are!

Everyone is unforgettable in their own special way. These are the things that each of us will always be remembered for.

_____

_____

_____

_____

_____

_____

_____

The Snowball Scoop!

There is no need to bundle up for this game because these snowballs are only made of cotton! The object of the game is to scoop as many snowballs as possible into a large bowl within one minute. The challenging part is that the players are BLINDFOLDED while doing it!

You'll need:

- bag of cotton balls
- large mixing bowl
- oversized serving spoon
- blindfold

Empty the bag of cotton balls into a pile on the floor and take turns doing "The Snowball Scoop." Encourage everyone to join in the fun and shout out directions to help guide the player. Tell them if they are "hot" or "cold" and cheer wildly, whether their snowball scoop is heaping full or completely empty. Either way, it's a hilarious sight!

Just Like Snowflakes, We're One of a Kind!

Our Winter Favorites

- Warm Beverage_____

- Board Game_____

- Craft_____

- Winter Scene_____

- Pen Pal_____

- Book to Snuggle Up with_____

- Way to Get Warm_____

- Indoor Sport_____

- Thing to Do When We Can't Go Outside_____

_____

*Laughter is the sun that drives winter
from the human face.*
Victor Hugo

What a Hoot!

*We really don't mind looking silly, it's true!
As long as it gives us a giggle or two.*

(Place photo here.)

Just for the Fun of It...

Dress-up photos can be lots of fun!

❦ Put on some peppy music and invite the kids to dress up Mom and Dad as Mr. and Mrs. Gigglebelly. Gather outlandish articles of clothing, scarves, jewelry, and hats, and then let the kids use their imagination. If Mom and Dad are really brave, they can let the kids create zany hairstyles and add freckles and rosy cheeks, too!

❦ Kids can be dressed up as snowmen using sweats stuffed with assorted pillows. Tie a bit of rope around the waist, then outfit them with a cap, muffler, and a black nose. Be creative! Then kneel and strike a silly pose.

Winter Housewarmings...

🍂 When the wind outside is howling, bring the fun indoors and play charades.

🍂 Treat the kids to a Maple Snow treat! Just pour heated maple syrup over a heaping bowl full of fresh fallen snow.

🍂 Snuggle up under quilts and blankets in front of a crackling fire and tell stories. (No fireplace? Mom and Dad's bed makes a cozy alternative.) Designate a storyteller and then let everyone contribute a word that must be used in the story. Record the stories for an unforgettable memory.

🍂 Put a kettle of soup on to cook and let it simmer slowly on the back of the stove, and when the family comes in from the cold they'll be greeted by its homey aroma. It will warm tummies with its nourishing goodness and fill hearts with happy winter memories.

🍂 Bring out old magazines and create a "Warm Winter Thoughts" collage. Use pictures and words that warm the heart with happy thoughts. Post the collages on the refrigerator or family bulletin board. All winter long the family will have happy thoughts whenever they need them.

🍂 Pop a big batch of popcorn and settle in for a cozy evening watching home movies.

Happy Birthday, Dear...

Guess who had a birthday!

_____

We celebrated by _____

_____

A Birthday Wish _____

_____

Guess who had a birthday!

_____

We celebrated by _____

_____

A Birthday Wish _____

_____

Our Winter Memories...

(PLACE MEMENTOS HERE.)